Walking in th[ ]
General Da..... ivurgan

Prepared for the United States Military Academy
at West Point, NewYork

by Robert Hampton, USMA Class of 1961
and George Schember

For information on the Winchester-Frederick County Historical Society, it's three museums, and other books published in the 85 year history, please email the Society at wfchs@verizon.net or contact the Society office at 1340 South Pleasant Valley Road, Winchester, Va 22601.

Cover: Daniel Morgan by Charles Willson Peale

ISBN # 978-1530609154

Printed in the United States of America

Contents

Portrait of General Morgan at Age 58,
      Philadelphia, PA (1794)
Current Burial Site, Mount Hebron Cemetery,
      Winchester, VA (1868)
Church & First Burial Site, Old Stone Presbyterian Church,
      Winchester, VA (1788)
First Home, "Soldiers Rest", Berryville, VA (1769)
Second Home, "Saratoga" Boyce, VA (1779)
Last Home, Winchester, VA (1800)
Burwell-Morgan Mill, Millwood, VA (1785)
Saratoga National Historical Park, Stillwater, NY (1777)
Battle Monument, Surrender Site, Schuylerville, NY (1887)
Cowpens National Battlefield, Chesnee, SC (1781)
General Morgan Monument, Spartanburg, SC (1881)
General Morgan's Sword, Richmond, VA
George Washington's Office Museum, Winchester, VA
Red Lion Tavern, Winchester, VA (1783)
Battletown Inn, Berryville, VA (1809)
Home of General Horatio Gates, "Traveller's Rest",
Kearneysville, WV (1773)
Kentucky / Pennsylvania Long Rifle
Congressional Gold Medal for the Battle of Cowpens (1781)
Society of the Cincinnati, Washington, DC (1783)
Cat of Nine Tails

INTRODUCTION

Daniel Morgan lived most of his life in the Winchester, Virginia area of the Shenandoah Valley. He was many things over his 66 years of life – frontiersman, wagoner, patriot, Indian fighter, farmer, businessman, miller, Revolutionary War hero, and U.S. Congressman. However, he deserves to be remembered the most for being one of the best American combat leaders during the Revolutionary War - an excellent tactician, superb leader of men, and outstanding light infantry commander.

He is best known for being the commanding general during the major American victory at the Battle of Cowpens, South Carolina, in January 1781. Cowpens was the turning point of the Revolutionary War in the South. The victory led eventually to the surrender of General Cornwallis and the British Army at Yorktown later the same year.

He was also a leader at the Battle of Saratoga in 1777. Saratoga is known as the turning point of the Revolutionary War. After the American victory and surrender of the entire British Army under General Burgoyne, the French decided to actively join the American cause. Although Horatio Gates and Benedict Arnold are the best known Americans at the battle, Colonel Morgan and his Virginia Riflemen fought in both battles and made a major contribution to the victory.

Morgan was tall, had broad shoulders and massive arms. The following is an extract from - *Daniel Morgan, Revolutionary Rifleman* (page vii): "Morgan joked, clowned, loved rum, enjoyed cards, took a common-law wife, and liked Indian attire. Without formal education, he spelled atrociously and lacked the prose style of 'pope, Voltiere, or Shakespear.' Preferring nicknames, he designated Washington as the 'old horse' and Cornwallis as the 'old fox." He himself was the 'old wagoner' or 'old Morgan." His friends were 'dear boys' - his enemies, 'raskels' and 'scoundrels.' He could be kind and tender. He could be pugnacious – his fiery temper and sensitivity to criticism involved him in innumerable brawls and lawsuits. If this man had his share of faults, mostly of temperament, they paled against his greatest virtue: loyalty – loyalty to his soldiers, his friends, and country. In Morgan's leathery face, with its prominent nose and forehead, firm mouth, and square chin, there was the appearance of rugged solidarity. Once he made a decision, he could be expected to stick to it. One had only to ask to determine his views on any issue. The American frontier movement produced few individuals as picturesque as Daniel Morgan."

After the war, a committee of the Congress set out to determine the service of those who had fought in the Revolution. They sent Daniel Morgan a questionnaire. He replied with typical directness – "Fought everywhere, was beaten nowhere."

CHRONOLOGY

<u>EARLY YEARS AND FRENCH AND INDIAN WAR</u>

1736 – BIRTH - Perhaps born of Welsh parents near Junction, Hunterdon County, NJ or nearby Bucks County, PA.

1752 – LEFT HOME (Age 16) – He left home probably after an argument with his step-mother - travelling west on the Great Wagon Road (current PA Route 30).   He worked odd jobs in Carlisle, PA and in Charles Town (current West Virginia).

1753 – WINCHESTER - Settled in Virginia near Winchester – farmer, sawmill superintendent, freight wagoner supplying western frontier settlements.

1755 – FRENCH & INDIAN WAR - Wagoner for the British Army. Served in General Braddock's expedition toward Fort Duquesne (now Pittsburgh) during the French and Indian War.

1756 – MILITIA - Private in Captain Ashby's Frederick County Militia.

1757 – REGIMENT - Commissioned ensign in George Washington's Virginia Regiment. Shot in the face by Indians at Hanging Rock, Virginia (now West Virginia).

1759 – BERRYVILLE - Moved to home near Berryville, VA.

1763 – ABIGAIL - Daniel and Abigail Curry set up housekeeping. Their first daughter, Nancy Morgan, was born on August 19, 1763.

1769 – NEW HOME - Daniel and his wife, Abigail Curry Morgan, rented a home in Berryville which was named "Soldiers Rest" after his harsh experiences in the Quebec campaign in 1775. Began farming.

1771 – MILITIA - Appointed as a militia captain.

1773 – MARRIAGE - Daniel and Abigail were married.

1774 – DUNMORE'S WAR - Had grown his farming operations to include 10 slaves. Commissioned captain in Virginia militia. Served in Dunmore's War, taking part in Shawnee Indian raids in the Ohio country.

REVOLUTIONARY WAR

1775 – QUEBEC EXPEDITION (Age 39) – Commissioned by Congress as a captain in the Continental Army. Virginia Riflemen (Morgan's Riflemen) from Frederick County. Marched from Winchester to Boston in 21 days to answer the call from George Washington. Morgan's 96 member Rifle Company was one of the first 10 companies in the U.S. Army. Leader of the vanguard on Benedict Arnold's unsuccessful expedition to Quebec. Taken prisoner December 31, 1775. Offered a colonel's rank by the British, but he indignantly refused it. Contracted sciatica on the arduous march to Quebec – low back and leg pain from pressure on the sciatic nerve.

1776 – PAROLED - Paroled by the British in August 1776. Commissioned Colonel of the 11th Virginia Regiment

(Morgan's Rifle Corps) on November 12, 1776 (designated the Seventh Virginia Regiment September 14, 1778).

1777 – BATTLE OF SARATOGA - Led the Virginia Riflemen during the major American victory at the two Battles at Saratoga, New York, September 19, 1777 and October 7, 1777.

1778 – BATTLE OF MONMOUTH - Was with the Army at Valley Forge and surrounding area for a short period during the harsh winter of 1777-1778. His unit was near but not directly engaged in the Battle of Monmouth Courthouse on June 28, 1778.

1779 – RESIGNATION - Resigned/Retired from the Army and returned home. Congress persuaded him to accept an "honorable furlough" until "something offers."

1780 – RETURN - At the request of General Gates and the Congress, rejoined the Army in the Southern Campaign. Promoted by Congress to brigadier general in the Continental Army on October 30, 1780. Began construction of his new home called "Saratoga" in 1779 or 1781.

1781 – BATTLE OF COWPENS - Commanding general during the major American victory at the Battle of Cowpens, South Carolina, on January 17, 1781. Soon after the battle, retired to his home near Winchester because of ill health - sciatica, and recurring bouts of malarial fever – until July. Awarded the Congressional Gold Medal for the victory at Cowpens on March 9, 1781.

1782 – NEW HOME - Completed construction of new home, "Saratoga."

1783 – RETIREMENT - Retired to "Saratoga."

LATER YEARS

1793 – MILITIA (Age 57) – Appointed major general in command of the Virginia Militia.

1794 – PORTRAIT - He sat for his portrait by Charles Willson Peale in Philadelphia.

1795 – LAND - By 1795, had acquired 100,000 acres in current West Virginia. His total possessions that year allegedly amounted to 250,000 acres, a large part of which was in the Northwest Territory (Ohio, Indiana, Illinois).

1796 – WHISKEY REBELION - Commanded the Virginia Militia ordered out by President Washington to suppress the Whiskey Rebellion in the Pittsburgh, Pennsylvania area.

1797 – CONGRESSMAN - Elected and served one term in the U.S. House of Representatives from First District of Virginia (March 4, 1797 to March 3, 1799) as a Federalist. At that time the Congress was located at Independence Hall in Philadelphia, PA.

1798 – HEALTH - Declined to be a candidate for re-nomination due to ill health.

1800 – NEW HOME - Purchased and moved into the house on Amherst Street in Winchester with his wife (Abigail), daughter and son-in-law (Betsey and James Heard) for last two years of his life because of declining health and to be near his Doctor (Dr. Daniel Conrad) and Minister (Reverend William Hill). Built an addition to the house.

1802 – DEATH (Age 66) – Died on July 6, 1802, in the upstairs bedroom of the house on Amherst Street in Winchester. He was buried at the Old Stone Presbyterian Church where he was a member in his later years. His remains were moved to the Mount Hebron Cemetery in

Winchester on July 13, 1868. Abigail died on May 18, 1816. *Saratoga* was declared a National Historic Landmark in 1973.

PLACES TO VISIT

WINCHESTER, VIRGINIA AREA

Current Burial Site, Mount Hebron Cemetery, Winchester, VA (1868). Located at 305 East Boscawen Street, Winchester, VA 22601. Phone 540-662-4868. The burial site of Daniel Morgan is through the main gate, left on Morgan Avenue, 250 feet down the road to the burial site on the right.

Church & First Burial Site, Old Stone Presbyterian Church, Winchester, VA (1788). Located at 306 East Piccadilly Street, Winchester, VA 22601, Phone 540-662-3824. General Morgan attended the church in his later years. A statue of General Morgan was erected on the corner by the Morgan Rifle Company.

First Home, *Soldiers Rest*, Berryville, VA. Located on the north side of Berryville near the intersection of Route 340 and the Route 7 bypass. Can be seen from the highway. Address P.O. Box 1224, Berryville, VA 22611. Privately owned, by Carl and Eileen Stephanus. Open by appointment, Phone 540-955-0703.

Second Home, *Saratoga* Boyce, VA (1779). Located on the west side of County Route 723, one half mile south of Boyce, Virginia. Cannot be seen from the highway. Privately owned by Page Mitchell. Not open to the public.

8

Last Home, Winchester, VA (1786). Located at 226 Amherst Street, Winchester, VA 22601. Privately owned and not open to the public. General Morgan died in the home on July 6, 1802.

Burwell-Morgan Mill, Millwood, VA (1785). Located in Millwood, Virginia 22646. Phone 540-837-1799. Website www.shenandoahvalley.com The historical marker nearby reads – "This Grist Mill, built in 1782-85 by General Daniel Morgan of Saratoga and Colonel Nathaniel L. Burwell of Carter Hall was in continuous operation until 1943. Now owned by the Clarke County Historical Association." Open to the public.

Hollingsworth Mill, Winchester, VA (1833). Located at 1360 South Pleasant Valley Road, Winchester, Virginia 22601. Phone 540-662-6550, Website www.winchesterhistory.org. Headquarters of the Winchester-Frederick County Historical Society. One of the items in their collecion is a small piece of wood from Daniel Morgan's original coffin removed from the cemetery at the Old Presbyterian Church.

SOUTH CAROLINA

Cowpens National Battlefield, Chesnee, SC (1781). Located at P.O. Box 308, Chesnee, SC 29323. Phone 864-461-2828, Website www.nps.gov/cowp/. Daniel Morgan is best known for being the commanding general during the major American victory at the Battle of Cowpens on January 17, 1781.

General Morgan Monument, Spartanburg, SC (1881). Located at Morgan Square in the center of Spartanburg. The Monument was established during the Centennial Anniversary of the victory at the Battle of Cowpens.

NEW YORK STATE

Saratoga National Historical Park, Stillwater, NY (1777). Located at 648 Route 32, Stillwater, NY 12170. Phone 518-664-9821 x224. Website www.nps.gov/sara/

NEW JERSEY

Roadside Historical Marker, New Hampton, NJ (1736). Located on Musconetcong River Road and reads - "MAJOR GENERAL DANIEL MORGAN, Commander of the Famed Morgan Rifle Corps, Born in this Village of New Hampton, Lebanon Township, NJ in 1736. Died in Winchester, VA July 6, 1802. Military Service French and Indian, Revolutionary War Battle of Quebec, Canada. Captured 1775. Distinguished himself in the Battle of Saratoga, NY 1777. Victor at the Battle of Cowpens, SC 1781."

PENNSYLVANIA

Valley Forge National Historical Park, Valley Forge, PA (1777-78). Located at 1400 North Outer Line Drive, King of Prussia, PA 19406. Phone 610-783-1077. Website www.nps.gov/vafo/ Daniel Morgan was at Valley Forge with the Continental Army for a short time during the harsh winter of 1777-78.

Independence National Historical Park, Philadelphia, PA. Located at 143 South Third Street, Philadelphia, PA 19106. Phone 215-597-8787. Website www.nps.gov/inde/ When Daniel Morgan served in the U.S. House of Representatives, it was located here in Philadelphia. They have the original first Charles Willson Peale (1794) painting of Daniel Morgan displayed in the Second Bank of the United States (1824).

OTHER

Fort Edwards, Capon Bridge, WV (1748). Located along the northern boundary of Capon Bridge, north of U.S. 50, 20 miles West of Winchester in current West Virginia. Website www.fortedwards.org. At Hanging Rock near the site, Daniel Morgan was wounded by Indians during the French and Indian War from a bullet through his neck and left side of his jaw.

City of Quebec, Quebec, Canada (1775). Located on the St. Lawrence Seaway in Canada, Website www.quebecregion.com. Site of the Revolutionary War Battle of Quebec, December 31, 1775. Daniel Morgan led the vanguard of the unsuccessful expedition and was taken prisoner.

PICTURES
PORTRAIT OF GENERAL MORGAN AT AGE 58 (1794)

**Portrait of General Morgan at Age 58, Philadelphia, PA
(1794).** Located at Independence National Historical Park,
Second Bank of the U.S., 143 South Third Street,
Philadelphia, PA 19106. Museum Phone 215-597-9373.
Website www.nps.gov/inde/.

The original first Charles Willson Peale painting of Daniel Morgan is on display at the Second Bank building in Philadelphia. At the request of his family, General Morgan sat for a second painting with Charles Willson Peale. In the first painting he is looking to his left. In the second painting he is looking to the right.

Virginia Historical Society, Richmond, VA. Located at P.O. Box 7311, Richmond, VA 23221. Phone 804-358-4901. Website www.vahistorical.org. The original second Charles Willson Peale painting of Daniel Morgan is located at the Virginia Historical Society.

2nd Portrait of Daniel Morgan by Charles Willson Peale

CURRENT BURIAL SITE, MOUNT HEBRON CEMETERY, WINCHESTER, VA (1868)

Current Burial Site, Mount Hebron Cemetery, Winchester, VA (1868). Located at 305 East Boscawen Street, Winchester, VA 22601. Phone 540-662-4868. The burial site of Daniel Morgan is through the main gate, left on Morgan Avenue, 250 feet down the road to the burial site on the right.

The wording on the stone is as follows -

> *"Major General Daniel Morgan Departed This Life on July the 6th 1802 in the 67th year of his age. Patriotism and Valor were the Prominent Features of his Character and the Honorable Services He Rendered to his Country During the Revolutionary War Crowned Him with Glory in the Hearts of his Countrymen a Perpetual Monument to His Memory."*

14

CHURCH & FIRST BURIAL SITE, OLD STONE PRESBYTERIAN CHURCH, WINCHESTER, VA (1788)

Church & First Burial Site, Old Stone Presbyterian Church, Winchester, VA (1788). Located at 306 East Piccadilly Street, Winchester, VA 22601, Phone 540-662-3824.

Scotch-Irish settlers built this stone meeting house for worship. General Morgan attended the church in his later years. A statue of General Morgan was erected on the corner by the Morgan Rifle Company. The wording at the base of the statue reads – "Fought Everywhere, Was Beaten Nowhere, Major General Daniel Morgan, Response Letter to Congress c.1798."

A roadside historical marker in Winchester reads –

GENERAL DANIEL MORGAN - Morgan used this Road in traveling from his home, "Saratoga," to Winchester. He was a Frontiersman, Indian Fighter and the Commander of Morgan's famous Riflemen in the Revolution. He won glory at Quebec and Saratoga, and defeated Tarleton at the Cowpens. He died in 1802 and is buried in Winchester.

FIRST HOME, "SOLDIER'S REST"
BERRYVILLE, VA

First Home, "Soldiers Rest", Berryville, VA (1780).
Located on the north side of Berryville near the intersection of Route 340 and the Route 7 bypass. Can be seen from the highway. Address P.O. Box 1224, Berryville, VA 22611. Privately owned, by Carl and Eileen Stephanus. Open by appointment. Phone 540-955-0703.

It is believed that Soldier's Rest was the home of Daniel Morgan before he built the large stone house he called "Saratoga" late in the Revolutionary War. Apparently, Daniel Morgan leased the farm and house and owned it briefly in 1800. Prior to the current house being built, a smaller one stood some 200 yards away, and is said to be the place where George Washington stayed when he was surveying the land here for Lord Fairfax in 1748.

The application for the National Register of Historic Places prepared by Maral S. Kalbian in January 1996, states that on May 6, 1800, Daniel Morgan purchased Soldier's Rest (per Frederick County Deed Book 27, page 51) and sold the property the following month (per Clarke County historian Curtis Chappelear in "Early Grants"). Maral also notes that Chappelear "acknowledged the possibility that Morgan leased the farm (Soldier's Rest) from its previous owner prior to 1800."

SECOND HOME, "SARATOGA", BOYCE, VA (1779)

Second Home, "Saratoga" Boyce, VA (1779). Located on the west side of County Route 723, one half mile South of Boyce, Virginia. Cannot be seen from the highway. Privately owned by Page Mitchell. Not open to the public.

The roadside historical marker reads – "SARATOGA – A half-mile east, Revolutionary War hero Daniel Morgan began this limestone Georgian mansion in 1779 while on furlough. He named it for the Battle of Saratoga in which he had recently distinguished himself. The house was probably constructed by Hessian soldiers held prisoner in nearby Winchester. Recalled to duty in 1780, Morgan was made a brigadier general and won a brilliant victory at Cowpens in South Carolina. In the antebellum period Saratoga was the home of Philip Pendleton Cooke, Virginia story writer and poet. It was later occupied by his brother, John Eston Cooke, historical novelist and biographer."

The following extracts are from - "Daniel Morgan, Revolutionary Rifleman": (page 172) "On his farm eleven miles from Winchester, he constructed a large two-story house, which he called "Saratoga." After borrowing a considerable sum of money from Thruston, Morgan began the work in 1780 or 1781, and completed it in 1782. Atop a rocky elevation, Saratoga today is almost obscured by trees as one approaches it on the old, narrow road that Morgan himself must have built. Valley tradition holds that much of the work on Saratoga was done by Hessian prisoners of war quartered near Winchester, these Germans reputedly carrying the stones in handcarts from the banks of Opequon Creek several miles away."

**LAST HOME
WINCHESTER, VA (1786)**

Last Home, Winchester, VA (1786). Located at 226 Amherst Street, Winchester, VA 22601. Privately owned and not open to the public.

The right side of the existing house on Amherst Street in Winchester was built in 1786, as more of a town house. Daniel Morgan purchased the house in 1800 and moved in with his wife (Abigail), daughter and son-in-law (Betsey and James Heard) for the last two years of his life. He was in declining health and wanted to be near his doctor (Dr. Daniel Conrad) and minister (Reverend William Hill). Needing more space, it is believed that he added the left side of the house. He died on July 6, 1802, in the upstairs bedroom on the right front of the house.

**BURWELL-MORGAN MILL
MILLWOOD, VA (1785)**

Burwell-Morgan Mill, Millwood, VA (1785). Located in Millwood, Virginia 22646. Phone 540-837-1799. Website www.shenandoahvalley.com. Open to the public.

The roadside historical marker reads -

> *THE BURWELL-MORGAN MILL - This grist mill, built in 1782-85 by General Daniel Morgan of Saratoga and Colonel Nathaniel L. Burwell of Carter Hall was in continuous operation until 1943. Now owned by the Clarke County Historical Association.*

The following is an extract from - "Daniel Morgan, Revolutionary Rifleman" (page 179):"A stone's throw away stands the old Burwell-Morgan mill, managed by Morgan while Burwell looked after a nearby store, which he operated. At times Morgan helped with Burwell's store, and the two men also seem to have run a distillery."

**SARATOGA NATIONAL HISTORICAL PARK
STILLWATER, NY (1777)**

Saratoga National Historical Park, Stillwater, NY (1777). Located at 648 Route 32, Stillwater, NY 12170, Phone 518-664-9821 x224, Website www.nps.gov/sara/.

The painting titled "Surrender of General Burgoyne" is shown in the picture above and was painted by John Trumbull in 1822. The original painting is at Yale University. Trumbull also painted an enlarged version which hangs in the U.S. Capitol Rotunda. Colonel Morgan is shown in the white uniform to the right center. He appears in front of the generals behind him because the painter, John Trumbull, apparently believed that the lower ranking Colonel Morgan had not received enough credit for the victory.

The Battle of Saratoga is known as the turning point of the Revolutionary War. It actually consisted of two battles fought in the same general area – Battle of Freeman's Farm fought on September 19, 1777, and the Battle of Bemis Heights on October 7.

After the American victory and surrender of the entire remaining British Army under General Burgoyne (6,000 men) on October 17, the French decided to actively join the American cause.

Although Horatio Gates and Benedict Arnold are the best known Americans at the battle, Colonel Morgan and his 500 Riflemen from Virginia, Maryland and Pennsylvania fought in both battles and made a major contribution to the victory. They were chosen individually by Colonel Morgan for their sharpshooting ability.

BATTLE MONUMENT, SURRENDER SITE
SCHUYLERVILLE, NY (1887)

Battle Monument, Surrender Site, Schuylerville, NY (1887). Located at 648 Route 32, Stillwater, NY 12170. Phone 518-664-9821 x224. Website www.nps.gov/sara/.

The Battle Monument is located at the site of the surrender of the British Army at the Battle of Saratoga. The statue of Daniel Morgan is on the west side of the monument. He is facing west - representing his life on the frontier. The other statues include General Horatio Gates facing north – forever facing down the British advance, Philip Schuyler facing east overlooking his property and the village that bears his name, and Benedict Arnold's empty niche facing south – symbolic of eventually joining with the British.

COWPENS NATIONAL BATTLEFIELD
CHESNEE, SC (1781)

Cowpens National Battlefield, Chesnee, SC (1781).
Located at P.O. Box 308, Chesnee, SC 29323, Phone 864-461-2828, Website www.nps.gov/cowp/.

Daniel Morgan is best known for being the commanding general during the major American victory at the Battle of Cowpens, South Carolina, on January 17, 1781. Cowpens was the turning point of the Revolutionary War in the South. The size of the American force at Cowpens has been disputed. General Morgan's official report on the battle states – 800 Continentals and Militia. Later researchers have concluded between 800 and 1,900. The size of the British force was 1,150 seasoned veterans.

The battle was a complete victory for the Patriot force. The British losses were staggering - 110 dead, over 200 wounded, 500 captured – plus cannons, muskets, wagons, horses, supplies, unit flags, etc. Morgan lost only 12 killed and 60 wounded. As General Morgan later said (it was) – "a devil of a whipping." The victory led eventually to the surrender of General Cornwallis and the British Army at Yorktown later the same year.

The painting titled – "Battle of Cowpens" was painted by Don Troiani. MD and VA Continentals surge into the British 7th Regiment of Foot, also known as the Royal Fusiliers, seizing both the unit's colors in hand to hand combat.

**GENERAL MORGAN MONUMENT
SPARTANBURG, SC (1881)**

General Morgan Monument, Spartanburg, SC (1881). Located at Morgan Square in the center of Spartanburg.

The monument was established in 1881 during the Centennial Anniversary of the victory at the Battle of Cowpens.

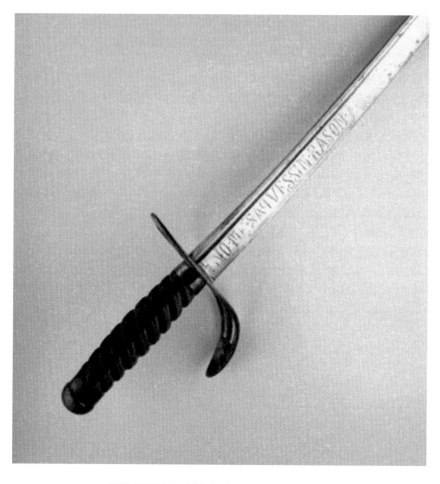

GENERAL MORGAN'S SWORD
RICHMOND, VA

General Morgan's Sword, Richmond, VA. Located at the Virginia Historical Society, P.O. Box 7311, Richmond, VA 23221. Phone 804-358-4901. Website www.vahistorical.org.

The sword was imported from Spain and was a common sword in the 1700s. The inscription on the sword blade reads – "Do not draw me without reason or sheath me without honor."

The following are extracts from - "Daniel Morgan, Revolutionary Rifleman" (page 49) regarding Daniel

Morgan's surrender at the Battle of Quebec: "The frustrations of being blocked at every turn by his fellow officers and of failing to gain the city swelled up in Morgan. Seeing the men around him throw down their arms, he burst into tears of rage. With his back against a building, he dared the British to try and take his sword. When they threatened to shoot him, he told them to go ahead. He refused to listen when his riflemen begged him to give up. Suddenly he sighted a priest in the milling crowd. In desperation he handed the surprised man his sword, saying angrily, "Not a scoundrel of those cowards shall take it out of my hands." (Note – The sword shown in the picture above is probably a later sword, not the one surrendered in Quebec.)

**GEORGE WASHINGTON'S OFFICE MUSEUM
WINCHESTER, VA**

George Washington's Office Museum, Winchester, VA. Located at 32 West Cork & Braddock Streets, Winchester, VA 22601, Phone 540-662-4412, Website www.winchesterhistory.org.

RED LION TAVERN
WINCHESTER, VA (1783)

Red Lion Tavern, Winchester, VA (1783). Located at 204 South Loudoun Street, Winchester, VA 22601. Now a gift shop and open to the public.

The tavern was frequented by Daniel Morgan.

**BATTLETOWN INN
BERRYVILLE, VA (1809)**

Battletown Inn, Berryville, VA (1809). Located at 102 West Main Street, Berryville, VA. 22611.

The Battletown Inn was originally built as a private home for the daughter of Berryville's founder. There was an earlier tavern about one and a half blocks away, on the northwest corner of Main and Charles Streets. It was replaced by a building that is now Sponseller's Flower Shop at 2 West Main Street. The legend is that Daniel Morgan, who reportedly liked to fight after he had been drinking, would leave piles of rocks on the road between his home at Soldier's Rest and the tavern. This gave him ammunition to throw at anyone who may have chased him home after a brawl at the tavern.

GENERAL HORATIO GATES' HOME
"TRAVELLER'S REST"
KEARNEYSVILLE, WV (1773)

Home of General Horatio Gates, "Traveller's Rest", Kearneysville, WV (1773). Located south of Kearneysville, West Virginia on Bower Road, one mile on the right side of the road. It is visible from Bower Road.

Gates and his family sailed from England to Virginia in 1772 and bought 659 acres on the Potomac River near Shepherdstown in what is now West Virginia. He built this limestone house and became a slave owner, a local justice, and a lieutenant colonel in the militia and a Revolutionary War general. In 1790, he sold the home, freed his slaves and moved to New York City. Daniel Morgan visited Traveller's Rest and his old war friend a number of times.

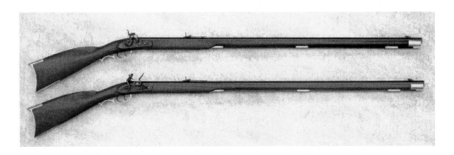

KENTUCKY / PENNSYLVANIA LONG RIFLE

Kentucky / Pennsylvania Long Rifle.

Most of Morgan's Virginia Riflemen carried Kentucky/ Pennsylvania long rifles. Originally developed in the 1730's, the long rifle was designed to meet the unique needs of the American frontier. Built lighter, sleeker, and firing smaller caliber ball than their heavier, more unbalanced European counterparts, the long rifle was not only more accurate but used less gunpowder and lead – both of which were scarce commodities in early America. Its effective range was over three times that of the British 'Brown Bess' smoothbore musket, which helped make both the American 'long rifle' and the frontiersmen who carried it legends in their own time.

The following are extracts from - *Daniel Morgan, Revolutionary Rifleman*: (page 19) "These veteran hunters and Indian fighters had traveled long distances without provisions and displayed remarkable 'dexterity' with the rifle. In shooting matches they desired targets at least 200 yards distant, preferably no larger than an orange. Contemporary accounts indicate that Lee did not exaggerate their marksmanship. Some observers even credited the frontiersmen with hitting objects at 250 yards or more. (A musket ball fell harmlessly to the ground at half that distance.) Whatever the truth, the Kentucky rifle, as it was called, was a deadly weapon in the hands of an expert. Spiral grooves inside the barrel, making the bullet rotate in flight, gave it range and accuracy.

Despite the advantages of the long, slender rifle, it did have serious limitations. While muskets could be fired four or five times a minute, riflemen were fortunate to deliver two shots in that time. Thus they found it difficult to stop a determined attack by their firepower, and they had not learned how to attach bayonets to their guns. Though unable to stand against a bayonet charge in open fields, they would be valuable as snipers and wood-fighters."

(page 76) "Though the value of the Kentucky rifle in the War for Independence has often been overstated, the weapon was an important factor in the two American victories on Bemis Heights, as Burgoyne and several officers pointed out in their memoirs" (Battle of Saratoga).

**CONGRESSIONAL GOLD MEDAL
FOR THE BATTLE OF COWPENS (1781)**

Congressional Gold Medal for the
Battle of Cowpens (1781).

Awarded to General Morgan on March 9, 1781, by the Continental Congress for the Battle of Cowpens. It was the fifth medal to be awarded. The citation reads as follows: "In recognition of 'fortitude and good conduct' displayed by Brigadier General Daniel Morgan and the officers and men under his command, in the action at Cowpens, in the State of South Carolina on January 17, 1781. Approved March 9, 1781."

It is not known if the original medal still exists or where it is. In 1973, this is one of the first 10 medals awarded by Congress to be reproduced and reissued in pewter by the U.S. Mint.

The following is an extract from - *Daniel Morgan, Revolutionary Rifleman* (page 184): "As the years passed, Morgan complained more and more about these ailments. Between 1790 and 1793 he spoke of being confined much of the time. This trying period was momentarily brightened for him by the belated arrival of his Cowpens medal, nine years after Congress had voted to give the award. The Revolutionary medals were made in France and brought to America by Thomas Jefferson in 1789. Morgan's was solid gold. Designed by the prominent artist Augustin Dupre, it bore the likeness of a general leading his troops in battle."

When General Morgan died in 1802, the medal was passed to his grandson, Morgan Neville - who was the bank cashier at the Farmers & Mechanics Bank of Pittsburgh. He kept the medal in the bank vault. On April 6, 1818, the bank was broken into and the gold Cowpens medal was among the items that were stolen.

SOCIETY OF THE CINCINNATI, WASHINGTON, DC (1783)

Society of the Cincinnati, Washington DC (1783).
Headquarters located at the Anderson House, 2118
Massachusetts Avenue, NW, Washington, D.C. 20008.
Phone 202-785-2040. Website ww.societyofthecincinnati.org.

The Society was founded in 1783 to preserve the ideals and
fellowship of the American Revolutionary War officers and to
pressure the government to honor pledges it had made
to officers who fought for American independence. Daniel
Morgan became a member of the Virginia chapter of the
society. The emblem of the Society is the eagle shown in
the picture above. The headquarters houses a museum and
research library.

The name "Cincinnati' comes from Roman Lucius Quinctius Cincinnatus who was a Roman Consul and Dictator of early Rome. He was a hero of Rome and a model of Roman virtue and simplicity. His abandoning of his work to serve Rome, and especially his immediate resignation of his absolute authority with the end of the crisis, has often been cited as an example of outstanding leadership, service to the greater good, civic virtue, and modesty. As a result, he has inspired a number of organizations and other entities, a number of which are named for him – including the Society of the Cincinnati.

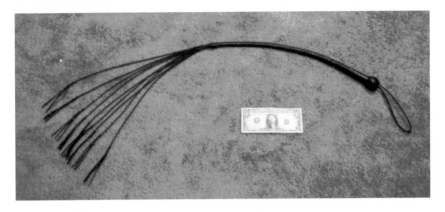

CAT OF NINE TAILS

Cat of Nine Tails

It is a type of multi-tailed whipping device that originated as an implement for severe physical punishment, notably in the Royal Navy and Army of Britain and used during Colonial times. The British Army had a similar multiple whip, though much lighter in construction, made of a drumstick with attached strings.

When the French and Indian War began, Daniel Morgan (age 19) was hired as a civilian by British General Edward Braddock for his ill-fated expedition to Fort Duquesne in 1755. In the spring 1756, while Morgan was taking supplies to Fort Chiswell, he irritated a British lieutenant who struck him with the flat of his sword. He then knocked the officer out with one punch. For that he was court-martialed and sentenced to a severe beating of 500 lashes (by a drummer at the camp whipping post). 500 lashes was far beyond the number that would kill most men.

Daniel survived but had severe scaring on his back. He later always maintained that the drummer had miscounted, and he had only been given 499 lashes, so the British still 'owed him one more lash.' During the Revolutionary War, when his soldiers asked him why he had such a hatred of the British Army and British officers, he would take off his shirt, turn his back to them, smile and walk away.

STORIES

EARLY LIFE

General Morgan rarely spoke of his early life and little is known of it. According to family tradition, however, he was born in 1736, in the area of Junction (now Hampton) in Bethlehem Township, Hunterdon County, NJ or in nearby Bucks County, PA. Today, a number of Morgans trace their lineage to Zachariah, the illegitimate son of Hannah Morgan, who they claim was the sister of Daniel Morgan. Under this scenario, which thus far has been documented, including the use of DNA evidence, Morgan's parents would have been James Morgan and Patience Perminter. There would have been eight children in the family. His mother died when he was 12, and when he was 16 or 17, he left home perhaps following a disagreement with his stepmother.

After working at odd jobs in Pennsylvania, he moved to the Shenandoah Valley and finally settled on the Virginia frontier, near what is now Winchester, VA. He worked clearing land, in a sawmill, and as a wagoner (teamster.)

He later served as a rifleman in the Provincial forces assigned to protect the western border settlements from French-backed Indian raids. Sometime after the end of the war, he rented a farm located between Winchester and Battletown (now Berryville). In 1774, he served in Dunmore's War taking part in raids on Shawnee villages in the Ohio country. He fell in love with Abigail Curry, and they had two daughters, Nancy and Betsey.

WOUNDING

The following is an extract from - *Daniel Morgan, Revolutionary Rifleman* (page 7): "In April 1756, Morgan guided a militia contingent from Fort Ashby to Fort Edwards, twenty miles north of Winchester. He and another ranger started back to Fort Ashby on the 16th. Fourteen miles out, seven Indians sprang from ambush and opened fire, killing Morgan's companion. A musket ball tore into Morgan's neck and passed out through the cheek, dislodging several teeth. Morgan wheeled his horse about and spurred back toward Fort Edwards. Six of the Indians stopped to scalp the dead man, leaving the seventh to overtake the fleeing Morgan. But Morgan had the faster mount; as he widened the distance between them, his pursuer threw his tomahawk but missed. Delirious from pain and shock, Morgan was still astride his animal on entering the fort. The wound, though not serious, left a permanent scar on his face."

DANIEL'S WIFE - ABIGAIL CURRY MORGAN

Like most great leaders, Morgan was helped and shaped by his wife, Abigail Curry Morgan and their family. The following are extracts from – *Daniel Morgan, Revolutionary Rifleman*: (page 11) "Plain, sensible, and pious,' she possessed some education and an interest in religion, both of which she reputedly passed on to Morgan. In the 1760's she bore him two daughters, Nancy Morgan (Neville), and Betsey Morgan (Heard), whom she educated herself until Morgan employed a tutor."(page 15) "Perhaps it was Thruston who persuaded Morgan and Abigail to be married in 1773, a step which Abigail may well have advocated for some time."

(page 100) "How Abigail Morgan had managed the farm in his absence is not apparent, but Morgan maintained that she underwent numerous difficulties....Despite her best efforts, Morgan found that his farm demanded attention."

(page 184) "Whatever Morgan's marital transgressions, he appreciated the good home Abigail made for him and the care she gave him during his sciatic and rheumatic difficulties."

MARCH FROM WINCHESTER TO BOSTON

In 1775, Daniel Morgan became the commander of one of two Virginia companies requested to be formed by the Continental Congress and to be sent to Boston to participate in the siege of the British Army in the city. The company of 96 men left for Boston on July 14, travelled the 600 miles in the mid-summer heat, and reached Cambridge near Boston on August 6. This was an average of 25 to 30 miles travelled per day. It is believed that they travelled on horseback. According the historian, B. Floyd Flickinger, their route was as follows:

July 14 – Left Winchester. Camped one mile south of Shepherd's Town (now West Virginia).
July 15 – Crossed the Potomac River.
July 17 – Arrived in Frederick, MD.
July 17-18 – Marched through German settlements of York, Lancaster, Reading, Allentown, PA (probably crossing the Susquehanna River at Harrisburg).
July24 – Arrived and camped in the Moravian town of Bethlehem, PA.
July 25-26 – Crossed the Delaware River at Easton and moved into northern NJ.

July 27 – Arrived at Sussex Court House, NJ and marched to the North River.
July 28-30 – Crossed the Hudson River at Peekskill, NY.
July 31 – Arrived at Milford, CT.
Aug. 2 – Arrived in Farmington and Harford, CT, crossed the Connecticut River and arrived in Coventry.
Aug. 3 – Arrived in Mansfield and Ashford, CT.
Aug. 4 – Arrived in Rhode Island.
Aug. 6 – Arrived in Cambridge, MA (Sunday evening). The second company of Virginians arrived several days later.

General George Washington, who was riding about the camp, saw the hardy band of his fellow Virginians and stopped. Captain Morgan, stepping forward and saluting, said, "General, from the right-bank of the Potomac." General Washington, overcome with emotion, dismounted and walked along the line of riflemen, shaking hands with every man. Then, mounting his horse, he touched his hat in salute and rode away without a word. Daniel Morgan, the old wagoner and Indian fighter, had not failed him.

TARGETING BRITISH OFFICERS

Daniel Morgan developed a hatred of the British Army and British officers. This related to his experiences during the French and Indian War, particularly the lashing he received during the Fort Duquesne campaign. In 18th century Europe, it was the generally accepted practice not to target officers in combat. Morgan encouraged his men to target the officers which was effective, causing chaos from the loss of officer leadership and direction on the battlefield.

The following is an extract from - *Daniel Morgan, Revolutionary Rifleman* (page 209): "Perhaps Morgan more than any other patriot officer typified the difference between British and American military practices during the Revolution. With a tradition of frontier combat behind him, he emphasized the thin skirmish line and individual marksmanship; the British, the bulky linear formation and volley fire. Morgan encouraged his sharpshooters to pick off enemy officers, whereas a kind of gentleman's agreement existed in European wars to spare the opposing leaders. As an Indian fighter, Morgan had concluded that there was nothing cavalier about war; it was an ugly business with one's chances of winning enhanced by crippling an opponent in any way possible, not by following time-honored rules and customs."

TURKEY CALL

The following is an extract from - *Daniel Morgan, Revolutionary Rifleman* (page 67) regarding the Battle of Saratoga on September 19, 1777, at Freeman's farm: "Morgan heard the shooting and crashed forward to discover what had happened. Certain that Morris's haste had led to the destruction of part of his corps, he became furious. Reputedly breaking into angry tears, he exclaimed to Colonel James Wilkinson, who had ridden up, 'I am ruined, by God…..my men are scattered God knows where.' Fortunately Morgan had his turkey-call. The sharp whistle enabled the riflemen to determine his location, and soon they gathered around him. Lucky to have lost few if any men, Morgan regrouped his corps and moved within sight of Freeman's farm, then occupied by Burgoyne's column."

The rest of the story as told by the staff at the Saratoga National Historical Park is as Follows: Morgan led the charge into the woods at Freeman's farm but ran into heavy fire from a line of British troops. Morgan and his men retreated. Morgan said in effect – "There I go, I did it again." (Like at Quebec when Morgan led the charge only to find himself ahead of the main body of troops - the British surrounded him and he was captured). Concealed in the tall grass, he let out his famous turkey-call to find out how many men he had left and where they were. He heard returned turkey-calls all around him from his men also concealed in the tall grass. Apparently, the new men had followed Morgan into the woods. The veterans who were with Morgan and taken prisoner at Quebec remained where they were in the tall grass and did not follow him into the woods.

RETIRED AND RETURNED DURING THE WAR

In 1779, during the war, Colonel Morgan resigned/retired from the Army and returned home. The Army was forming a new corps of light infantry. Anthony Wayne of Pennsylvania was appointed as the commander, rather than Daniel Morgan. The appointment also included a promotion to brigadier general. Appointments and promotions to general officer were approved by Congress. In addition, the number of generals was allocated by colony based on the number of men serving in the army from each colony. All of the general positions authorized for Virginia were filled.

The following letter he wrote and personally delivered to Congress in Philadelphia: "From these considerations I could not but flatter myself, that if at any time a respectable corps of light troops should be formed I should be honored with the command of it....I am however disappointed, such a corps has been formed and the command of it given to another – As it is generally known that I commanded the light troops of our army and that the command is now taken from me, it will naturally be judged that this change of officers has taken place either on account of some misconduct in me, or on account of my want of capacity. I cannot therefore but feel deeply effected with this Injury done my reputation.....I can with sincerity declare that I engaged in the service of my country with a full determination to continue in it as long as my services were wanted. I must conclude from what has happened, that my country has no more occasion for me, I therefore beg leave to retire."

Congress persuaded him to accept an "honorable furlough" until "something offers."

Colonel Morgan returned to the Army in 1780, to participate in the Southern Campaign where he was promoted to brigadier general on October 30, 1780.

RELATIONSHIPS AND OPINIONS OF OTHERS

The following are extracts from - *Daniel Morgan, Revolutionary Rifleman*:

George Washington (page 79) – "of all the officers he ever served under, Morgan respected Washington the most." In a letter from Washington to Morgan at the beginning of the Saratoga campaign Washington said (page 61) "I know of no Corps so likely to check.....(Burgoyne's) progress in proportion to their number, as the one you Command. I have great dependence on you, your Officers, and Men."

Marquis de Lafayette (page 79) "No officer took a keener interest in the riflemen than a recent arrival from France, the Marquis de Lafayette, a tall young man who wore the epaulets of an American major general.....Morgan, the crude frontiersman, and Lafayette, the polished nobleman, became fast friends."

Otho Williams (page 180) – 'Of his many army friends, Morgan treasured Otho Williams most.....Far from being rough and hearty like Morgan, Williams was a frail man, usually in ill health, whose tastes ran to scholarly subjects, especially classical literature. Each man found the other refreshingly different."

Horatio Gates (page 113) – "but after he (Gates) moved to New York City in 1790, the warmth between the two Saratoga veterans melted; the reason is obscure but may well have been because of politics, since Gates was as ardent a Republican as Morgan was a Federalist."

Nathanael Greene (page 155) – "Greene, a canny judge of

men, recognized Morgan as one subordinate he trusted to operate independently at a great distance from his own encampment and very near that of the enemy…..As the Rhode Islander remarked after Morgan left the Southern army, 'Great generals are scarce – there are few Morgans to be found."

Benedict Arnold (page 40) – "Differences they had, but Arnold could count on Morgan's loyalty and co-operation. Even after Arnold's treason brought him national execration, Morgan could remember the swarthy little man as 'my old friend."

Anthony Wayne (page 97) – "Although Morgan admitted that Wayne outranked him, he pointed out that his military experience exceeded the Pennsylvanian's. Wayne was 'still enjoying the sweets of domestic life' while he had fought two Indian wars."

Thomas Nelson (page 166) – "Trifles' never won wars. The Governor (Nelson) considered Morgan a man of sound sense who, in his brusque way, had a knack for getting to the heart of a problem."

LAST DAYS

The following is an extract from - *Daniel Morgan, Revolutionary Rifleman* (page 213):
"But (Reverend) Hill and Lemuel Brent, another Winchester friend, observed that Morgan believed God had forgiven him for his follies of earlier years and that he faced death with the same courage he had displayed throughout life. Mentally he retained his old vigor. Subsequently a neighbor remembered 'verbatim' a conversation between the patient and his physician during the last days. 'Doctor,' said the General, 'if I could be the man I was when I was twenty-one years of age, I would be willing to be stripped stark naked on the top of the Allegheny Mountain, to run for my life with a

pack of dogs at my heels.' But the past was gone. Morgan died on the morning of July 6, 1802, at the age of sixty-six."

MOVING BURIAL SITES

The historical marker at the Mount Hebron Cemetery states – "Attempted removal to his New Jersey birthplace in 1865 was blocked by disinterring and hiding the remnants, as well as the vandalized gravestone, until reburial in the Mount Hebron Cemetery in 1868. A second threat of removal came in 1951 when a delegation from Cowpens, South Carolina came to the cemetery."

The following is an extract from - *Daniel Morgan, Revolutionary Rifleman* (page 214):
"But within 100 years, visitors might have wondered whether the local citizens had ever heard of their old hero. Morgan's remains had been removed from the original burial location, the local Presbyterian graveyard, for fear Yankee soldiers would carry them away during the Civil War; they were reinterred in Mount Hebron Cemetery in 1868. His gravestone, already chipped and blurred, became more difficult to read. And as the cemetery expanded, the older part where Morgan's casket lay was no longer properly attended; grass grew up around the General's marker.

Then, in July 1951, Winchester was rudely awakened. At Spartanburg, South Carolina, a city near Cowpens battlefield, the chapter of the Daughters of the American Revolution enlisted the aid of other civic groups to remove the General's remains to their community, where they would be accorded more respect than at Winchester. But when a Spartanburg delegation with picks and shovels appeared at Mount Hebron Cemetery in Winchester, a startled caretaker called the police. Soon a crowd of Winchester 'patriots' gathered at the cemetery, determined to keep what was rightfully theirs. Outnumbered, the South Carolinians retreated home. *Life* magazine described the incident in a lively article titled, *'Who Gets the General's Body?'*

(Note - The article appeared in the September 3, 1951 edition of *Life* magazine. The article states that support for Cowpens was given by General Morgan's great-great-granddaughter, Mrs. Josephine Callahan of Redwood City, California. She wanted a more imposing grave built for her ancestor.)

In the end, Morgan's memory was the victor, for the Winchester-Frederick County Historical Society erected an impressive granite monument bearing the General's likeness over the grave. Unveiled by children descended from members of Morgan's first rifle company, it was dedicated by Congressman Burr P. Harrison. Even in death, Morgan was the center of activity and not a little controversy."

MOVIE (2000) – *THE PATRIOT*

Netflix has rated *The Patriot* first on its top ten list of the most patriotic movies. Amazon.com has rated it third. *The Patriot's* producer, Mark Gordon, said that in making the film, "While we were telling a fictional story, the backdrop was serious history." The film's screenwriter, Robert Rodat, said of Mel Gibson's character: "Benjamin Martin is a composite character made up of Francis Marion (The Swamp Fox), Daniel Morgan, Thomas Sumter, and Andrew Pickens, and a few bits and pieces from a number of other characters."

Possibly, the parts related to Daniel Morgan are Benjamin Martin in the movie (1) fighting Indians during the French and Indian War and Dunmore's War, (2) targeting officers during his guerilla raids, (3) fighting in the Battle of Cowpens at the end of the movie.

The final battle was inspired by the battles of Cowpens and Guilford Courthouse. The Americans used the same tactics in both battles. In the film, the name of the battle, as well as the winning side, was taken from the Cowpens battle. The sizes of the armies, as well as their being led by generals Greene and Cornwallis, come from the Guilford Courthouse battle. The scene where Cornwallis orders his artillery to "concentrate on the center," during which they killed both Continentals and his own troops, took place at Guilford Courthouse.

DESCENDANTS

As mentioned earlier, much of Morgan's ancestry is a mystery. Under the current Morgan family research, there would have been eight children.

(1) Catherine Morgan
(2) Elizabeth Morgan.
(3) Daniel Morgan
(4) David Morgan
(5) John Morgan.
(6) Hannah Morgan
(7) James Morgan.
(8) William Morgan.

We have a much clearer view of Daniel Morgan's family which had two daughters, (Nancy and Betsey) with his wife Abigail Curry and one illegitimate son (Willoughby) mother unknown.

NANCY MORGAN (NEVILLE)

Nancy Morgan was born August 19, 1763 and died February 18, 1839 (age 75). She married Presley Neville (a Revolutionary War Veteran) on October 15, 1782 at age 19, and they had 14 children over a period of 25 years.

(1) Morgan Neville – named for his grandfather Daniel Morgan
(2) Emily Morgan Neville (Simms).
(3) Fayette Neville (Wilkins) – probably named for Lafayette.
(4) Betsey M. Neville (O'Hara) – named for Nancy's sister Betsey.
(5) Nancy Neville (Reed) – named for her mother Nancy.
(6) Francis Neville.
(7) Presley John Neville – name for his father.
(8) Winifred Neville (Gee).
(9) Edgar Neville.

(10) Ellen Neville (Byrn).
(11) Frances Scott Neville (Foster) – probably named for Francis Scott Key.
(12) Clarence Montague Neville.
(13) Frederick Augustus Neville.
(14) Mortimer Neville.

BETSEY MORGAN (HEARD)

Betsey Morgan was born in 1765 and died in 1813. She married James Heard (also a Revolutionary War Veteran) on October 17, 1785, and they had four children.

(1) Daniel Morgan Heard – named for his grandfather Daniel Morgan.
(2) Morgan Augustus Heard – also name for his grandfather.
(3) Nancy Morgan Heard – named for Betsey's sister Nancy.
(4) Matilda Heard (O'Bannon)

WILLOUGHBY MORGAN

The following is an extract from - *Daniel Morgan, Revolutionary Rifleman* (page 183):

"It is not generally known that Morgan also had a son. Born in the mid-1780's, Willoughby Morgan was illegitimate, and his mother's identity remains a mystery. His birth so embarrassed Morgan that he never referred to Willoughby in his surviving letters or in his will. Apparently at a very early age Willoughby was sent to South Carolina, where he grew up and studied law. By 1811 he lived in Winchester and later raised a company of infantry in the War of 1812. Compiling an impressive combat record, he decided to make a career in the army, rising to the rank of lieutenant colonel. A woman who knew Willoughby declared that he possessed considerable formal education and like his father, was tall and muscular. After serving at western posts in Indiana and Wisconsin, he died in 1832."

None of Daniel Morgan's descendants are believed to currently live in the Winchester, Frederick / Clarke County, Virginia area.

RESOURCES

BOOKS

Daniel Morgan, Revolutionary Rifleman - by Don Higgenbotham. 1961. Institute of Early American History and Culture in Williamsburg, and University of North Carolina Press. 1961. The most authoritative book on Daniel Morgan.

The Life of General Daniel Morgan of the Virginia Line of the Army of the United States - by James Graham. 1856. The first biography of Daniel Morgan. The author married a great-granddaughter of General Morgan and had access to a body of the General's papers that remained in the family.

Daniel Morgan: Ranger of the Revolution – by North Callahan. 1961. Ams Pr Inc. The second biography of Daniel Morgan.

A Devil *of a Whipping: The Battle of Cowpens* - by Lawrence E. Babbit. 1998. University of North Carolina Press, Chapel Hill, NC. The most authoritative book on the Battle of Cowpens.

ORGANIZATIONS

Winchester-Frederick County Historical Society. Located at the Hollingsworth Mill, 1360 South Pleasant Valley Road, Winchester, VA 22601. Phone 540-662-6550. Website www.winchesterhistory.org.

Clarke County Historical Association. Office and museum located at 32 East Main Street, Berryville, P.O. Box 306, Berryville, VA 22611. Phone 540-955-2600, Website www.clarkehistory.org. Own and operate the Burwell-Morgan Mill.

Cowpens National Battlefield. Located at P.O. Box 308, Chesnee, SC 29323. Phone 864-461-2828, Website www.nps.gov/cowp/

Saratoga National Historical Park. Located at 648 Route 32, Stillwater, NY 12170. Phone 518-664-9821 x224, Website www.nps.gov/sara/

Valley Forge National Historical Park. Located at 1400 North Outer Line Drive, King of Prussia, PA 19406. Phone 610-783-1077. Website www.nps.gov/vafo Daniel Morgan was at Valley Forge for a short time with the Continental Army during the harsh winter of 1777-1778.

Independence National Historical Park. Located at 143 South Third Street Philadelphia, PA 19106, Phone 215-597-8787. Website - www.nps.gov/inde/ Has the original first Charles Willson Peale (1794) painting of Daniel Morgan displayed in the Second Bank of the United States building.

Virginia Historical Society. Located at P.O. Box 7311, Richmond, VA 23221, Phone 804-358-4901, Website – www.vahistorical.org Has the original second Charles Willson Peale painting of Daniel Morgan and General Morgan's sword.

New York Public Library. Theodorus Bailey Myers Collection. Has General Morgan's original papers.

Society of the Cincinnati Library. Headquarters located at the Anderson House, 2118 Massachusetts Avenue, NW, Washington, D.C. 20008. Phone 202-785-2040. Website www.societyofthecincinnati.org

PEOPLE

George and Jeanne Schember – Co-author of this document. President, Winchester-Frederick County Historical Society. Also live in and own the last home of Daniel Morgan in Winchester. Address 226 Amherst Street, Winchester, VA 22601. Phone 540-667-2559, Email: schemjg@verizon.net

Bob Hampton – Co-author of this document. Address 4201 Oakridge Lane, Chevy Chase, MD 20815. Phone 301-907-2613. Email rhamptonlrg@aol.com

Terry L. Morgan, Sr. - Direct descendant of Hannah Morgan, Daniel Morgan's sister.

Carl and Eileen Stephanus – Current owners of "Soldiers Rest" home. Address - P.O. Box 1224, Berryville, VA 22611. Phone 540-955-0703. Email cstephanus@earlthlink.net

Kathryn Lynn – Superintendent, Cowpens National Battlefield, Phone 864-461-2828. Email:kathryn_lynn@nps.gov.

Page Mitchell – Current owner of "Saratoga" home.

Jim Hughto (Hudo) – Tour Guide at Saratoga Battlefield. Phone 518-235-8550.

Karie Diethorn – Chief Curator, Independence National Historical Park Museum Collection. Phone 215-597-9373. Has the original first Charles Willson Peale painting (1794) of Daniel Morgan.

OTHER

Movie (2000) – **The Patriot**. Starring Mel Gibson. His fictional character is a composite of Francis Marion (The Swamp Fox), Daniel Morgan, Thomas Sumter, and Andrew Pickens. The final battle was inspired by the Battles of Cowpens and Guilford Courthouse.

45INDEX

D

F

G

H

N

O

P

34430395R00036